Real Estate Agents and Loan Originators

Full-Hearted Focus

The antitode to exhaustion is full heartedness.
~ David Whyte

By Joe Stumpf

Full-Hearted Focus

By Joe Stumpf
Copyright ©2014 by Joe Stumpf
All rights reserved. First edition 2014

No part of this book may be reproduced in any form without the prior written permission of the author. Reviewers may quote brief passages in reviews.

Published by By Referral Only, Inc. 2035 Corte Del Nogal, Suite 200 Carlsbad, CA 92011 www.byreferralonly.com

What's Inside Full-Hearted Focus

How To Get Focused……………………..…….. 5

How To Stay Focused……………………….…14

How to Get Others Focused……………………21

How to Get Money Focused……………………32

About Joe Stumpf………………………………59

How To Get Focused

What does it mean to you to have focus?

What do you feel like when you have focus?

What questions do you ask yourself when you are focused?

What would your life look like if you were two times more focused?

And what is the opposite of being focused?

What does it feel like when you're not focused? Are you distracted? Confused? Unclear? All three?

I know that when I'm not focused I feel overwhelmed, stressed and conflicted.

How about when you *are* focused?

I feel purposeful and determined, excited and at peace. How about you?

Remember a time when you were in a high state of focus. What did it feel like?

When I sat down to write this little book, I was thinking about focus. It was 1pm on a Saturday afternoon and I only had about 90 minutes before my daughter Tracy arrived to leave for a wedding.

So I went onto my porch with my journal and everything I had already collected on the concept of focusing. I also flipped on the TV because I wanted to hear what my Padres were doing against the Milwaukee Brewers.

I could feel my attention being pulled in a few directions. I was pressured by the deadline of the project, my self-interest in the game and my commitment to being on time for the wedding.

After about 20 minutes of struggling to get my thoughts together, I got focused. I turned off the TV, I went downstairs into my writing sanctuary and I completed the first draft of my thoughts on focus in the next 70 minutes.

So what did I do to double my productivity? Really three things:

1) I focused on one thing.
2) I had a clear goal with a deadline.
3) I eliminated all distractions.

Focusing On One Thing

You might have heard me say that it's far more productive to focus on one thing 100% of your time with 100% of your energy rather than spending 10% of your energy and 10% of your time focusing on ten different things.

That's why I always ask: **What is the one thing I can get done in the next 30 days that will have the biggest bottom line improvement in my business over the next 12 months?**

The question I ask is: *What is the one thing I can get done?*

Try that question on. What one thing can you get done in the next 30 days that will have the biggest bottom line improvement in your business over the next 12 months?

Take some time to really think about the answer because this is where you'll pour all of your energy and time into.

If I was sitting next to you right now, I would act like a magnifying glass. I would have a clean yellow pad in front of us and I would write down these words: What is the one thing you can get done in the next 30 days that will have the biggest impact on your business over the next 12 months?

Then I'd write five words vertically on each line:

        1) Leads.
        2) Appointments.
        3) Contracts.
        4) Closings.
        5) Referrals.

Leads, appointments, contracts, closings and referrals.

I'd put my hand on your right shoulder, look you in the left eye (which is the window to you soul) and magnify the importance of these focusing questions:

Do you have a system to produce a consistent, predictable number of leads?

If you have enough leads coming into your business in a consistent, predictable manner, do you need a reliable system to convert those leads to appointments?

If you have a reliable appointment creation system, do you have dialogue mastery and systems in place right now to convert your appointments to contracts?

If you have enough listings, buyers and loan applications, then do you have enough structures in place to get those listings sold, your buyers into homes and your loans closed? If you said yes, do you have a reliable, predictable referral-generating system and structure in place?

What you may or may not notice is the biggest mistake people make is trying to work on all five words at the same time and never getting any systems in place.

As you consider the benefits of being focused on one thing, you might like to pick one focus area for 30 days. Will you focus on generating leads?

Will you focus on generating appointments? On contracts? Closings? Or referrals?

You may have already started to become aware of what happens to your mind when you pick just one. If you pick the right one, you feel peaceful. If you pick the wrong one you feel confusion and stress.

For example this past Friday at my home during one of the breaks in our dialogue school, one of the young guys working with me asked me to help him get focused. Because focus is so important to achieve higher levels of success, I actually took out my magnifying glass just to signify the need to focus. I'm sitting next to this young man and in my hands is a magnifying glass.

I asked him: What one thing can you get done in your business in the next 30 days that will have the biggest improvement on your bottom line results over the next 12 months.

Is it lead systems?
Is it appointment systems?
Is it contract systems?
Is it closing systems?
Is it referral systems?

Without much thought he said, "I need closings."

"How does that feel?"

"I feel anxious," he said.

I asked him, "When you feel anxious, what's the thought you're having?"

"I'm anxious because I'm thinking about the fact that I have no clients right now and I need closings."

"I suggest that you pay close attention to this feeling," I said. "Then become aware of the thought that's causing the feeling and let the feeling act as a guidance system to determine if the thought is directing you towards the proper goal."

I then asked him what it feels like to think about building a lead-generating system that gets him anywhere from 20 to 25 prospects a month. I watched a smile come across his face. And he said, "It feels good."

"What are you thinking when you say you're feeling good?" I said.
"If I had 20 to 25 leads a month, I would have enough appointments to get one to two closings a month and that's what I really want," he said.

I just love the thought that you can determine where you need to put your focus in the next 30 days.

For many of you, it's leads. How does that feel when you think about building a system in the next 30 days that generates leads?

For some of you, it's appointments. How does that feel?

For a few of you, it's contracts. That means you already have enough appointments and leads. What you have to do is convert your current appointments to contracts.

A few of you have enough listings, buyers and applications for loans. You don't need any more leads or appointments but you need to convert what you have right now to closings.

For the rest of you, it's referrals. So imagine just working on a lead-generating system for 30 days. Imagine that. We talked about being single focused. Make the single focus for the next 30 days to create a system that will generate 25 leads a month. What does that feel like to have that focus? Get rid of everything else. Get rid of all of your distractions and set up one system that generates 25 leads a month.

A really great By Referral Only member, Jacqui Dobens, has her sister put up 50 to 60 Ugly Yellow Signs on Saturday morning at 6am all throughout her geographical area in the Los Angeles area. Then they take them down Sunday at 6pm. She's been doing that every Saturday for about six months. The results of that single focus is she has created a reliable system that gets her four appointments a week from her Ugly Yellow Sign system.

In order to get four appointments, she needs to generate about 25 leads. Once she had that system in place, she could work on converting the appointments to contracts, the contracts to closings and the closings to referrals. But she could only focus on one part of it at a time.

So what is that one thing? One thing you can get done in the next 30 days is build a system that will produce the biggest bottom line results in your business over the next 12 months.

What does it feel like when you think about having one thing done in the next 30 days that will improve the bottom line results in your business over the next 12 months? It's a very powerful question because you have to focus on yourself.

You have to focus on creating long-term sustainable results yourself.

I would highly recommend that you sit down with your journal and pen in a quiet place – no TV, no computer, no email, no radio, no refrigerator – and put all your attention on just one thing.

If you could pick one thing from the following five goals and you knew you could not fail, which one of these would you pick?

1) Generate 25 leads in the next 30 days.
2) Convert 50% or more of your current leads to appointments in the next 30 days.
3) Convert 50% of your current appointments to contracts in the next 30 days.
4) Convert 70% of your current contracts to closings in the next 30 days.

5) Get 50% of the people in your During Unit to refer you during the process.
6) Create a process that gets a 20% referral rate from your After Unit.

Imagine right now you picked one of these goals. Imagine you will be beheaded if you don't pick just one and put all your focus on it. With that goal on the top of your page and in the top of your mind, make a list of all the things you can do in the next 30 days to make that goal come true.

This is a great exercise to do with your coach, in your mastermind group or by yourself quietly in a distraction-free environment. The great thing is you have plenty of productive things you can do in any one of these five areas to achieve your goals.

There is no shortage of strategies, especially with By Referral Only using our Before, During, and After library of systems. The absolute secret is to focus only on one thing at a time with five things to choose from at any given time.

So pick one. Is it to generate leads? If you have enough leads, is it to convert your current leads to appointments? If you have enough appointments, is it to convert those appointments to listings, buyer broker agreements or loan applications? If you have enough buyer broker agreements, listing and loan apps, is it to convert those contracts to closings? Is it to get your listings sold? Is it to get those buyers a home? Is it to get those loans closed? Or is it to create a system where 50% of people refer you during the process and approximately 20% refer you or repeat with you in the After Unit? Which one is it?

Going forward from here, look at your business every day and ask yourself which of the five bankable results you will focus on.

Now if you're in a safe place, I want you to really concentrate with me for just a minute. I want you to just relax.

As you relax and your mind slows down it becomes easier to pay close attention to your thoughts and to where your mind goes. Notice that each thought and each sensation seems to stand out to become bigger than before the same way tiny images become enlarged when viewed through the lens of a magnifying glass. Examine things in detail. Don't miss a thing. Be aware of each word.

Focus in as I begin to explain that you can pay close attention to whatever you need to, whenever you want to by quieting down and zeroing in and becoming still inside like this.

As your mind finds it easier to be aware of one thing at a time, like listening to me and examining every detail, you start to enjoy discovering how it all fits together. Sticking to a job, seeing it through, dealing with every detail right to the end becomes easier over time as your mind begins to play with its own ability to just stay put.

Be intently still as you realize how easy it is to continue doing so. Be aware that your mind can comfortably stare at anything at all, absorb it and enjoy it.

As you continue to hear the sound of my voice and the meaning of my words, each word lets you know even more than before that you are paying attention fully using a magnifying lens you can use anywhere at all. Focus. Focus on one thing at a time.

   Is it to generate leads?
   Is it to convert leads to appointments?
   Is it to convert current appointments to contracts?
   Is it to convert current contracts to closings?
   Is it building a During system to get a 50% referral rate?
   Is it creating an After Unit to generate a 20% yield?

You can only magnify one thing at a time. Which one will it be for the next 30 days?

In the next chapter we will examine how to sustain your focus over long periods of time.

But for now, you're going to pick one thing to focus on for 30 days.

You can do it.

Do it!

How To Stay Focused

What's the possibility you will stay focused on that one system until it is completely built and yielding predictable results? Well if you're like me you could sure use some help staying focused.

So let's talk about staying focused by setting up systems that make your business work. Now I know what you might be feeling right now or might be saying to yourself. *Joe, I need to get focused so I can set up the systems.*

I understand. We'll get into that in just a minute.

I have good news for you. I just finished my meditation and God told me he has a little message for you. It said that everything's going to be okay. Just stay focused.

It's like going into a candy store. If you try to eat all of it at one time you're going to get sick. Just pick one thing and enjoy it fully. And then when you're done, come on back. There's always going to be more time to work on what you want to work on.

Right now you have picked one system. And that's the way you get focused. The way you stay focused is dedicating three to five hours a week working on that one system. I call that Remodel time.

I'm not going to tell you that Remodel time is the secret to staying focused because you already know that.

You see, scheduling three to five hours a week to work on your business is the only activity that will give you the leverage you must have to get the joy, the peace and the freedom you so desire.

If you invited me to your office to sit down with you to help you get focused, we would first determine what system we'd work on.

Second, we'd pull out your annual calendar and cross off three to five hours a week for the next 52 weeks dedicated to working on your systems. It would be ideal if it was Monday from 9am to noon. Or if it was Thursday from 4 to 8 that would be just as good. If it was Monday one week and Friday the next week, that would be fine too. As long as you have five hours a week in your calendar dedicated to working on your business.

And that's the secret; *get it scheduled*. Nothing will bring you more peace, joy and freedom faster or more permanently than committing yourself to one year of three to five hours a week working on your business.

The third thing we would do is create an environment where you can be distraction-free.

This is a place where you can go for three to five hours a week without any distractions at all. Distractions are everywhere. The TV, the cluttered desk, the ding of the email when it's delivered, phone calls, text messages. I can go on and on. Everything around you can distract you.

So turn off the TV, clean off your desk, turn down the volume knob on your pc and have someone answer your phone so you can put all your energy into this one project. You get the idea.

Why don't you scratch down on a piece of paper three things that can distract you? Then identify what you can do right now to remove, eliminate or defer those distractions when you want to get focused.

Remember, focus and clarity are siblings. Both of them are required to get you greater results to come even closer to unleashing your fullest potential. I believe you have so much potential. We've got to get clarity and we've got to get focused to unleash that potential.

I have a sanctuary in my life. This is a place where I work distraction-free on our businesses. If you've been to my home, maybe to spend time at Dialogue School, you've spent time in my optimal sanctuary. That's the place where I work on the business. It's fully functional and it's completely distraction-free for me. If I were with you right now, what we would do is stop everything and create a similar environment for you.

You've heard me say 100 times, environment is always stronger than willpower.

You can have all the intentional willpower in the world, but it will still fail if your environment does not support it. Your willpower will never be as strong as the environment. It's so critical that you create an environment that supports what your will is.

The fourth thing we do is make a list of 100 things we want to do in our life and our business before we die. That's right. 100 things. This is essential because we need brain space.

I liken the brain to a hard drive. I need to get all the stuff that is on my brain onto paper so I can use my brain for processing rather than storage.

Something really powerful happens when you focus yourself and put 100 things on a piece of paper that you want to accomplish in your life and your business before you die.

It's like clearing off the hard drive. Your brain knows that the ideas are now safe because you've captured it on paper like prisoners and they're not going to escape.

The brain is now free to work on what is in front of you, not trying to remember everything you want to do. The secret is just to pour it all out of your brain without a sequence or priority. It might look like this:

I'm going to go to China.
I'm going to go to France.
I'm going to take my daughter to Italy.
I'm going to buy insurance for my car.
I'm going to change the light bulb in the bathroom.
I'm going to get my bills paid before I go out of town.
I'm going to find my sunglasses.

I'm going to save some money.
I'm going to get married.
I'm going to fall in love.
I'm going to race a car in Alabama.
I'm going to quit drinking coffee.
I'm going to write a best-selling book.
I'm going to speak to 10,000 people.
I'm going to hire Jack Trout to consult for me.
I'm going to have dinner with David Hawkins.

I could go on and on to list 200 or 300 things I want to do before I die. But you get the idea. Just go on a rampage and get it all out of your head. You will experience a new level of freedom and focus that you've never experienced in your life. Your brain will love it.

Your brain knows that its purpose is for processing, not storage.

If you choose to work on it, I recommend that you decide to work on your business in a very focused, directed way.

And in order to do that, you must decide in advance what you're going to be working on during your Remodel time. You don't decide what to do during Remodel time; you decide to do it before Remodel time.

Let's say you sat with me and said, "Coach, I'm going to be working on getting leads in my business."

I would say, "Okay, we can look in the Before Unit, the During Unit, the After Unit to generate leads. Let's make a list of all the things you can do and put it into a priority sequence."

Then you go to work on your business. You don't decide to do this while you're working on your business, you decide to do this beforehand.

Then the fifth thing I would recommend is the one that's probably the easiest and the one that will guarantee you absolute focus if you follow the instructions exactly.

Create a Mastermind group with two other BY REFERRAL ONLY members. Just two other members. I would highly suggest that you form a triad with two other equally-committed members who are focused on getting things done. For at least a dozen different reasons, three is the optimal size group for achieving significant results fast.

So after you're done reading this, find two other people who want to join you.

At your first meeting you'll agree upon the date and the time when you're going to meet on the phone. I suggest that you set up three-way calls. Ideally these are a 30-minute conversation right before you begin your Remodel time.

So if you've picked Mondays from 9am to noon, you are looking for two partners who will meet with you every Monday from 9-9:30. In that 30 minutes, each of you get 10 minutes to talk about what your goal is, what you've gotten done so far, what you are going to get done and what kind of support you need.

You each get 10 minutes. The call is done in 30 minutes. Keep these groups virtual. Meet on the phone or maybe in front of your computers. But please be efficient. The focus is on getting things done.

What is powerful is the size of your group being three people. When you get more than three people, one can miss and the others don't really care. But if you have three people, everybody has to show up. Everybody has equal accountability.

The next key piece is to only be with your group for six weeks and then form a new group. There's a certain level of focus that a group can contain for six weeks and then it starts to slack off. Then what you do is disband and get two new people.

Do that every six weeks, constantly finding two new people to keep you focused. I'll call that little group a triad or if you like a trinity. The secret is to put that group together and focus together for 30 minutes for six consecutive weeks on one project.

Before I wrap up this chapter I need to tell you about a blizzard a friend of mine drove through last winter. Now believe me, this is going to have a point. He left his home in Sacramento on Tuesday afternoon to drive to Reno. He wanted to go see his stepson play hockey and the game was on Wednesday so he drove up on Tuesday. It was real close to the end of the season. He hadn't been to any of the games and was feeling pretty guilty so he was willing to do whatever it took.

As he drove up into the foothills of the Sierra, a little light rain began to fall and the temperature was right around 52 so he thought he could make it no problem. As it got dark and he climbed into the Sierras, the temperature started to drop pretty sharply. First 46° then 40° and then 36°. He noticed snowflakes starting to fall in front of his headlights. Then he looked at the thermometer on his dashboard and he saw the temperature outside the car had dropped down to 29°.

There are no streetlights up in these mountains. The snow blocked the moon in his headlights and visibility closed in around him. There was darkness all around him and he said he could only see about 10 feet in front of him.

All he could see was the snow blurring in front of his headlights. But there were faint tire tracks ahead of him. They were dark stripes in the fresh snow on the ground. There's no lanes for visibility up there. And you get really close to the edge. If you've ever driven through the Sierras, you want to stay away from the cliff. It is a long drop. So he settled down and he just started following the red tail lights of the car in front of him.

And for about the next 50 miles the only way he could navigate was to keep his eyes on those two red headlights. He crept along 10 miles an hour for 50 miles.

He kept his eyes on those two glowing red tail lights of the car for five hours. I can only imagine how tedious that might have been. But it got him to where he was going.

And I know in your life and my life there are days that it seems like there's a blizzard. There are so many things going on outside of us and around us, but you just have to keep your eyes focused on your goal in order to get there.

Stay focused. Join a master mind group. Clean out your brain. Create an environment that's distraction-free and work on one thing at a time. And you will stay focused.

How to Get Others Focused

As a trusted advisor, one of the greatest gifts you can give is the gift of focus. I know that when I go from a state of confusion to a state of clarity, I feel empowered to take action. And when I'm focused, I'm motivated.

What does it feel like when you think about assuming the role of the person who motivates your clients into action by helping them get focused?

In this chapter you're going to learn how to focus your sellers, your buyers and your borrowers so they are motivated to take action. The way I see it, when you're working with a seller, a buyer and a borrower you're number one responsibility is to keep them focused.

I've put together what I call the five focal points for each: a seller, a buyer, and a borrower. These five focal points are the difference that makes the difference.

You may have noticed that agents and lenders often really lose their focus and start obsessing on minor things versus keeping all their energy on what really makes a difference. The five focal points are your responsibility. They keep your client focused.

As a matter of fact, you might want to consider yourself a focus-finder. The more that you can focus and refocus your sellers, buyers and borrowers on these five focal points, the more fun, joy and abundance everyone's going to experience.

So what are those five focal points?

First let's just talk about the seller and then we'll talk about the buyer and the borrower.

Seller focal point number one is to focus your sellers on their dreams, golas and values.

Take a quick look at each listing you have right now and ask yourself a couple questions:

1) Is each one of your current sellers crystal clear on what's important to them?

2) Can you actually look at each seller that you're currently contracted with and say out loud what their dreams, goals and values is?

3) Are each of your sellers being pulled with passion towards their dream?

4) Are you reminding each of your sellers obsessively throughout the entire transaction that their dreams, goals and values is the highest version of their dream?

5) Do you let your sellers know that when they slip into a lower version of themselves they've forgotten what is really important to them? I'm talking about when they start to bicker and negotiate things that are meaningless. They've forgotten what is really important to them.

6) Do you recognize your role in each of your seller's lives as the person who must keep them focused on what's important to them?

Seller focal point number two is to focus on the real value of their home.

Your role is to keep your seller focused on what they have control of, not what they don't have control of. They cannot control the economy, but they can have the most attractively-priced home in their category. And because

22

you have such strong focus for them on their dreams, goals and values, the seller is willing to look at the most creative ways to make their dream come true.

People cannot make their dream come true if they're not aware of it. So when someone asks you the question "What's my home worth?" the answer is always "to whom?"

You keep them focused on the fact that the house has no intrinsic value at all and that the only value the house has is what the person's willing and able to pay for it. The intrinsic value is in what a person will pay to own it, not what the seller wants or what they need.

The real question is, "How important are your (insert their goals, dreams and values) and how soon do you want to realize those dreams, goals and values?"

What I've noticed is the sacred cow that must be killed in real estate is that my home has intrinsic value. It doesn't.

Because of your skills at educating your seller, they now know that they don't determine what the home is worth unless they're willing to pay the price that they're currently asking. So ask them, "Would you pay what you want for your home right now, right here?"

Every client you now work with is becoming more aware. What I've noticed is a seller who is aware of what's important to them is 10 times more flexible than the seller who's unaware.

Focal point number three for the seller is to focus on being BIC: best in class.

You and I both know that when we're asked how the market is the answer is: "Tell me where you live and I can tell you how your market is."

The market is the exact number of homes that you're competing against in a geographical area that are similar in location, square footage and t offered at the same time in a same area. The market is great for homes that are best in class.

Look at each listing that you have right now. How many of your sellers are truly focusing on the diligence that it takes to be best in class? If there are 18 homes for sale in that same geographical area with the same square footage and time on the market, how many of your sellers are obsessed with being the best out of the 18?

Experience shows that the role of the BY REFERRAL ONLY consultant is to keep the seller focused on what they have real control over. And one thing they have control over is how much they're willing to invest in time and money to be best in class.

Seller focal point number four is getting the seller focused on removing all obstacles to getting their house sold.

Again, look at each one of your listings that you're servicing right now. How many of your sellers are truly focused on removing all the obstacles in the way of getting their home sold? Are they motivated to remove all those road blocks so they can get it sold?

For example, how willing are they to show their home? How much accessibility do you have? How quickly can you get into the home for a showing when a buyer wants to look at it? Are they willing to reschedule their life to make it for sale? Are they making the sale their highest priority? Do they have that mindset of being for sale 24 hours a day, 7 days a week?

How many of your sellers are truly focused on 100% willingness to get their home sold? Are your sellers supporting your ugly yellow sign program? How many of your sellers have fully appointed you as the expert at selling their home and recognize that they're the amateurs?

You've heard me say pros don't collaborate with amateurs just like doctors don't ask for patient advice before surgery. When your seller removes the obstacles they are letting you fully direct the logistics of the sale of their property. When they don't remove the obstacles, they're not giving you logistical control.

Have you focused your seller on removing obstacles so the home can get sold?

And then focal point number five for the seller is are they willing to help you get it sold?

As their consultant, your role is to focus your seller on the activities that they can do to make their dreams, goals and values come true.

Is your seller willing to hand out listing business cards at work? Is your seller willing to record and post a Facebook message describing the property to their friends?

Is your seller focused on communicating to neighbors that their home is for sale? Is your seller focused on helping you with neighborhood open houses?

Has your seller given you a list of everyone they know so they can send a flyer to them to see if any of them might know somebody who'd be interested in their home?

How willing is your seller to assist in financing for the new buyer? Is your seller focused on helping you get it sold?

So those are the five focal points for a seller.

Now let's look at the five focal points for a buyer.

Focal point number one for a buyer is getting the buyer focused on their dreams, goals and values.

Do you have a formal process to discover your buyer's dreams, goals and values before they see a home? Do you have a commitment to only show homes that will make your buyer's dreams, goals and values come true? The more committed you are to that, the less confusion they have.

Every time you're showing a home you can say, "This could make your (insert their dreams, goals and values) come true." Are you asking that every time your show a home?

The secret to motivating the buyers is always keep their dreams, goals and values in their consciousness at all times. That of course means you need to know their dreams, goals and values.

Buyer focal point number two: your buyer clients are focused on negotiating a price that makes their dreams, goals and values come true.

Have you focused your buyer on avoiding negotiating fever? That's when they get involved in mindless, senseless, petty negotiations that move them away from their dreams, goals and values instead of towards it.

When a buyer's not clearly discovered their dreams, goals and values, what is likely to happen is that they will slip into a low version of consciousness and look at every negotiation as a win-loss scenario. However when you make it your intention and focus all your energy on making the negotiations about their dreams, goals and values instead of the house, you quickly discover how much trust you have with your buyer.

Remember the speed of trust? When everyone trusts each other because everyone has told the truth, things move real fast. And when there's no or low trust, negotiations move very slowly if at all.

Focal point number three for a buyer: Your buyer client must have some pre-agreed process for looking at home and you must have a pre-agreed showing process.

A buyer can easily get overwhelmed and lose all their focus if the process of looking at homes is not organized and structured around making their dreams, goals and values come true. The human mind has the capacity to manage about seven plus or minus two bits of information simultaneously.

I'm not going to tell you that you'll never show more than 7 homes before you sit down with a buyer and do a careful analysis of what they've looked at because you know that's not true. But when you sit down and you revisit your dreams, goals and values, after you've shown them 7 homes, then you'll discover how close you are to the truth.

You know from experience that if you show more than 7 homes without doing a home-showing review, your buyer will feel overwhelmed and easily lose focus. And when people are out of focus, what they do is procrastinate, hesitate and isolate. The theme of showing homes is to find one to buy, not to show homes. Keep the focus on the process of buying, not just showing.

Focal point number four is to focus your buyer client on being fully responsible throughout the entire process.

Keep your buyer focused on the fact that the process of buying a home begins after they find one. Only about 20% of your energy and time is finding a home. Then you have to start the negotiations. Then you have to remove all the conditions. Then you have the whole celebration process. Then you add the 90-day process after the transaction is closed.

What is your focus on? Keep your client focused on the entire process, not just finding the home.

Focal point number five is getting the buyer client focused on your advice.

You're the leader. They look to you for what to do next. They delegate fully to you. You ask them to fully trust you. You do your homework so you know what's on the market. You know what their draeams, goals and values and you're always checking with them to see if they're still being guided by the dreams, goals and values that the two of you discovered together.

When a buyer starts to tell you what homes they want to look at, always go back to their dreams, goals and values and make sure that what they're interested in is their dream and not just the curb appeal of a new listing.

So those are the focal points for a buyer.

Now what about the focal points for a borrower?

Let's talk about the things you have to keep people focused on when they're borrowing money.

Focal point number one is that the borrower is crystal clear what their dreams, goals and values is.

Of course it all starts with this clarity of their dreams goals and values just like it does for sellers and buyers.

One of the most critical questions you can ask is, "What's important about the purchase of this home?" However when somebody's refinancing you might say, "What's important about the loan you're about to get?"

Lenders, listen carefully. It's absolutely essential to shift the conversation from a left brain discussion to a right brain life conversation. Otherwise you're just going to become a commodity. And the fastest way to do that is to wrap whatever advice you give to your client in their goals, dreams and values.

The key is to remember that you're not getting them a loan; you're helping them make their dreams, goals and values come true.

Focal point number two: focus your borrower on what is important about money.

It seems like the days of the loan hack are gone for good. Your new role is educating your client on college funding, reverse mortgages, debt management, debt reduction, credit worthiness and even some good investment strategies. The loan rate is not the focus of the conversation.

You must get your client focused on the full range of advice that you can provide. And this requires trust. Trust happens when you tell the truth. Money is very emotional. Just look at their FICO score. That reveals just how much emotional stability they have. You may be the only person on the planet that knows their credit worthiness.

Focus on making them think that you really care about their overall financial help, not just this loan. Even if you don't care, make them think you care until you do care. The more a client thinks that you care about the big life picture more than about their money, the more they will trust you.

To have this relationship is really worth going deep around the question, "What's important about money to you?" It will be very exciting for you to know what's important about money to them and also to know what's important about this next loan to them. You may have to go deep several different times to discover the highest version of themselves.

Focal point number three is to focus your borrower to be proactive in the process of handling all the paperwork.

This is an overwhelming area for many people. The less time you spend having them answer what I call situational questions like age, address, bank account numbers, Social Security numbers and all that stuff about their situation and the more time you invest on what's important to them, the more proactive they will be. When you capture all their situational information and store it all electronically, then you can fill out the forms and just verify to recheck it.

Focal point number four for a borrower is to focus your borrower on removing all the obstacles they have control over quickly and

effectively.

Can you make a list of the 10 biggest obstacles the majority of people are facing when they're funding their dream? Can you get into your client's skin and know how your client feels about getting a loan? How well do you really know your borrower? How well do you know them?

In my experience, money can create so much fear or it can create enormous joy, depending on what a person is feeling at any given moment. And when a client is in fear, it is best not to talk to them until they're out of fear. In my experience, when a person is in fear they forget about what's important and they drop into pure survival.

Focal point number five for a borrower is to keep them focused on your trusted advice.

They are focused on your leadership. They want your advice and they will follow it because you are a trusted advisor. My definition of a trusted advisor is a person who skillfully focuses their client on what is important and then keeps the client focused on what is important throughout the entire transaction.

How do you focus your client? Create trust and then give them the advice that will give their dreams, goals and values truth. Get addicted to making people's dreams, goals and values come true.

That means getting out of the real estate business, getting out of the mortgage business and getting into the dream-making business. Instead of being a salesperson, be a dream realizer. Be a person in whom people realize the highest version of themselves in your presence. Become absolutely engrossed in the process of helping people realize what is really important to them.

It's safe to say that most people have not taken the time or had anyone ever care enough to help them discover what's really important to them. Get addicted to the joy people feel when they have a profound experience like self-discovery. Get really addicted to the highest version of a person and you will watch them get focused and stay focused. Get out there and help people get what they want and I promise you'll get everything YOU want.

How to Get Money Focused

This chapter is something I've chosen to do based on my own personal experiences and my own principals that I have applied in my life to actualize a lot of money. My intention is to share with you my deepest truth about money in the hopes it will create an opening for you to have money flow freely into your life as it has for me.

It can take anywhere from 5 to 10 hours of thinking before I actually start to begin my writing. I will usually sit down with my notes and my journals and review years of writing about my life.

But something was missing when I prepared for this. It was a lack of language to describe the highest version of myself in regards to money.

Whenever I get stuck when I'm creating a lesson that I want to teach, I stop and I meditate. The meditation is usually on the outcome that I want you to have when you're done listening to this. So I chose to sit and meditate and allow whatever was to give birth in that meditation believing it would be the best information needed to serve you.

In my meditation I concentrated on imagining you reading this message. I saw you with the book in your hands. And I imagined that I was talking to you on a very personal level about my experience with money. I imagined you reading intently, taking notes and having that "aha" moment. I envisioned you having a very profound shift in your relationship with money.

What is Money?

Value is not in money.

Value is in human life.

I've recently read a wonderful book by Garrett Gunderson called <u>*Killing Sacred Cows*</u>. In his fabulous book he explains a concept that I've always wanted to put into language, but he really did a magnificent, elegant job describing what he calls human life value.

Human life value is everything we have to offer the world when we strip away all of our material possessions. It's our thoughts, our character and our unique abilities. Value is any act of meaningful worth or significant service that when valued by another creates joy for both parties.

Money is not power.

It's merely a representation of value. When you really think about money, money comes only in three ways. There's only three really clearly defined ways that you can get money.

1. Coercion. This is like Robin Hood. You steal it and then justify your act. You take from the rich and give to the poor. You coerce people.
2. Deception. You earn someone's trust and then violate it.
3. Add value. Value is any act of meaningful worth or significant service that when provided for and valued by another creates joy for both parties.

So how do you focus on making money? The answer is simply to ask yourself *what can you do to bring people value*? That's a question I'm constantly asking myself: what can I do right now to bring you value?

A number of years ago – actually it was back in 2003 – I got a call from my buddy Dean Jackson. He said, "I'm going to send something over to you." I took a look at what he sent and after I was done looking at it, I made a decision to write down what I really believed were the intrinsic things that create value for me and help me create wealth. So I wrote a series of letters to my nephew Air'n entitled: **"How I Make Money".**

I'm going to share all these letters with you now but before you read them keep in mind I wrote them is 2003 when my nephew was 19 years old. Eleven years after I sent these letters to him, Air'n has built three companies two of which he has sold for over 100 million dollars. His third company is valued over 300 million dollars. You can find out all about his business at inflection.com.

Letter 1

"Dear Air'n, a few hours ago my friend Dean Jackson and I were on the phone talking about a book he just received in the mail. His excitement about the book was unlike anything I've ever experienced from my buddy Dean. He told me that he was holding a 193-page book that resembled the Dead Sea Scrolls. He went on to describe a book that was a series of letters from Gary Helbert written to his son Bond. Gary wrote 30 letters in 30 days while he was serving a 10-month prison sentence for a crime he says he did not commit.

In his first letter he tells his son Bond that he is committed to writing for 60 minutes a day for 30 consecutive days sharing everything he knows about marketing. Now Air'n the name Gary Helbert might not mean much to you right now, but as you will discover when you study the great direct response marketers of all time Gary Helbert is in the top 5 of all time with people like Jay Abraham, Dan Kennedy, Claude Hopkins, and even Dean Jackson. Dean described these letters as 5 to 7 pages of handwritten text that detailed all of Gary's secrets of direct marketing success. That's like Popeye discovering spinach. As Dean described the book, the idea popped into my mind that the way that I could provide value for you is I could write one hour a day to you.

What I could share with you are my insights, my awarenesses, my strategies and my learnings that I have experienced during the last 20 years of business. So my commitment to you is to share from my heart what I did, what I didn't do, what I'd do differently, what I wouldn't do differently, how I would do it and why I did it. I'd like this to be a valuable text. A series of letters that you could use as a blueprint for your personal success and a model of what you can do for somebody someday.

Imagine Air'n, you writing for one hour a day describing how you achieved your success and your significance in your life in the same format.

As you read these letters, think about paying it forward and you'll know what I'm talking about.

Knowing your appetite to learn and your developing willingness to give, I'm sure you will do the same for another as I'm going to now do for you.

So my first lesson is entitled 'Think and Grow Rich'. I bought this in 1983 as my first book by Napoleon Hill.

I still have that book sitting on my desk at home. Right now I'm at Starbuck's in Encinitas writing this letter to you. That's where I just bought this journal I'm writing in. Air'n, the secret that Napoleon Hill shares at least a thousand times in a hundred different ways is that whatever the mind of man can conceive and believe, he will achieve. When I first read those words in 1983, I had little reverence for the power of those words.

Today in my evolution, which has been more spiritual, I might say that whatever the mind of man can conceive and believe with prayer, it will be achieved. Prayer in this context means vigilantly asking God to reveal how my dreams and aspirations can be of service and add value to others.

In 1983, I wrote some words in a journal that spoke my highest vision at that time. I wrote, 'I am the highest paid, most sought-after speaker in the world.' And I wrote those 11 words over a thousand times over the next 10 to 15 years. I wrote it like this: Joe Stumpf, you're the highest paid, most sought-after speaker in the world. Joe Stumpf, you're the highest paid, most sought-after speaker in the world. You, Joe Stumpf, are the highest paid, most sought-after speaker in the world. The highest paid, most sought-after speaker in the world is Joe Stumpf. Air'n, I filled my journals with that mantra, believing that through repetition and constantly bombarding my brain with this simple affirmation that all the resources would be revealed to me. And the more I internalized that statement, the more it would come true.

I took Tom Hopkins' picture and Zig Ziglar's picture and I framed them. Then I took my picture and framed it and put it right next to theirs. And the reason I did that was these two men were both model speakers, both highly sought after and highly paid and making millions and millions of dollars a year. Having pictures of people who have achieved what you desire to achieve helped make it more real. And it still does that for me today.

Air'n, the affirmation that I am the highest paid, most sought-after speaker in the world is just loaded with ego. I see that today. At the time I wrote it, I knew no other way. I was completely obsessed with a goal.

Now let me tell you what was driving my drive. **Because that's lesson number two. There is always a drive behind the drive.** You see Air'n, my little brother Robbie died when I was 21 years old. When Robbie was 10, he came to me and asked me if I would take him to a track meet at school. Now imagine that a 10-year-old boy wanted me to take him to a track. He wanted to learn how to run and jump and all kinds of things. And I promised him that I would drive him to this track meet on Saturday morning.

Well Saturday morning came and we had to be there by 9am. Robbie was up at about 7am with great anticipation that his older brother Joey would be there to have this great day with him. Well, here's what really happened. The night before I got so drunk that I passed out in my car in the bar parking lot. I woke up at 8:30, still drunk, stinking like a skunk. I rushed over to the house and Robbie was on the porch and he was in tears.

I stumbled out of the car and ran up to him. He said, "Joey if we hurry, we can make it." I looked at Robbie and said, "Rob, I don't have any gas in my tank." "We can stop and get some," he said.

Then I said the words that haunted me for the next 15 years. I said, "Robbie, I don't have any money for gas." And he looked at me in shock. How can my big brother let me down so badly?

Then I said, "Can I borrow $5 dollars from you?"

Get this picture. I'm 20 years old. I'm a real estate agent. I was always touting how great I was and here I was drunk at 8:30 in the morning asking my 10-year-old brother for $5 bucks for gas so I could keep my promise to take him to a track event.

Well Robbie, this little saint, reluctantly went upstairs and went into his piggy bank and came back with three dollar bills and a pocket full of change totaling $5. We went to the gas station. I got $3 worth of gas and a pack of Marlboros. I hid the cigarettes in my pocket with embarrassment.

We made it to the track event and it was a very somber day. Over the next three weeks, Robbie asked me for the $5 bucks back at least a dozen times and I never had it. Three weeks and four days after the track meet, Robbie died in a tornado accident.

When I went to his funeral, I made a vow that no matter what I will always have money. That no matter what, I could always pay my own way. That was my drive behind my drive. Air'n, after several thousand dollars in therapy and countless hours of working through this issue, my drive to succeed has evolved.

I have made amends with Robbie, but the truth remains. To achieve extraordinary results you must have a strong enough *why* to endure.

Well, it's about 10:30 now and it's time for me to go home. I'll continue tomorrow. My lesson number one is: 'Think and Grow Rich'. And lesson number two is: 'Know Your Drive Behind Your Drive'.

Love, Your Uncle Joey.

Letter 2

"Air'n, I'm sitting on my deck overlooking the Pacific Ocean with a Cuban cigar and a fresh Starbuck's ready to give you 60 minutes of mentoring. I hope this letter finds you as happy as I am on this very wonderful evening. Now just to review our first lesson 'Think and Grow

Rich' is to discover the power of repetition of an affirmation. And lesson number two is 'The Drive Behind the Drive'. Whenever you see financial success in a person, you can bet they have a powerful *why* that motivates them not to be mediocre. Read Lance Armstrong's book *It's Not the Bike*.

Tonight I want to share with you a winning formula. The concept of a winning formula comes from Werner Erhard. Werner started a personal development self-awareness movement in the 1970's called EST. And EST is Latin for 'what is'.

It was at the EST seminar in 1982 that I heard Werner Erhard explain the concept of the winning formula. A winning formula is the internal belief you have about yourself that gets set early in your life about life and how you get what you want. We all have a winning formula. Some people have a formula called 'I'm a victim' or 'I'm better than you' or 'I got more than you' or 'I'm smarter than you' or 'I'm the smartest person in town' or 'I know more than you do'. I'm sure by the end of this letter you will be close to knowing what your winning formula is. My formula is 'I'll get you before you get me.'

This winning formula is a two-edged sword. It can serve me and it can also sabotage me. In competitive situations I can actually experience my body transform into 'I'll get you before you get me'. This has been a very instrumental part of gaining wealth for me.

The reason is that when you start to make money, you quickly discover that money has a certain energy that reveals the ego or dark side of ourselves. Money activates fear and greed and pride and guilt and shame. That's why I believe when it comes to money, trust only God not people.

Most people lose all their power and turn to force when big money is at stake. Big money activates the dark side of the winning formula.

My winning formula is 'I'll get you before you get me' which assumes someone is trying to get me. This means I shift from love to fear. Being aware of your winning formula helps you recognize the winning formula others operate from.

Since the accumulation of wealth always requires the exchange of money from one person's pocket to another, you will always be dealing with your own winning formula or someone else's. By helping me understand what my winning formula was, Werner Erhard raised my consciousness to the point that I'm very aware of when I am coming from 'I'll get you before you get me'.

As a result, when I attract people into my life in this fearful state of mind, they are usually attacking me or that is what I am projecting onto them. The result is that I counterattack. When I am coming from fear, it is always ego-driven.

The ego loves conflict. Money always has a way of creating conflict because so much ego is attached to having it, getting it, spending it, saving it, hoarding it and adoring it. So my lesson for you is this. When you're dealing with money, especially big money, it has an energy that calls forth the ego in ways you could never imagine. Remember, the opposite of ego is God. And God is love. In the Bible, the word money appears more frequently than any other word because God knows money is the fastest way to connect to the ego. And it will pull you into fear.

I remember one afternoon my brother Johnny said to me when I was in the midst of a money conflict, 'You've made dead presidents your god.'

I'm aware Air'n that you will be very financially successful. The way I have done it is by changing my formula over the last 20 years from 'I will get you before you get me' to 'I will give to you before you give to me'.

This simple shift from 'get' to 'give' is the shift from fear to love. From ego to God. Again Air'n, this level of awareness is not common in most people. And of course most people don't make big money, but they do have big egos. Maybe you can even think of professors at the campus that have a big ego but no money.

So Air'n, what's your winning formula? Think about your underlying beliefs about money. Maybe it's to prove to your folks that you can do it. Or to have your folks know that you're not stupid.

Remember that whatever your formula is, your dark side and your shadow is revealed by money.

John O'Neil wrote an epic book called *The Paradox of Success*. I actually hired John for a day to personally coach me to better understand my toxicity around success. John told me, 'Confidence has a shadow called arrogance.' In other words the more confident you become, the more arrogant you can be. The shift to make is that the more confident you become, the more vigilant you must keep your humility. Intelligence has a shadow called infallibility. And many times I was wrong, but because I thought I was so smart I lost a lot of money, both in the stock market and in business.

The shift you must make is to understand that the more you know, the more you realize what you don't know. These are priceless lessons because making big money is actually simple. It's really only about giving value, creating value or being of value. Whatever you do that has value, money will always follow. So work on being a valuable person who seeks to give value to people. I'm in the coaching business and whenever I give advice I always follow it up with a question, 'Is that of value to you?'

Air'n, I encourage you today to start making your number one goal in every interaction with every human being to bring them value. And then ask, 'Did you receive value?'

You will quickly learn that value is only received once it is recognized. Often what we perceive to be of value is not recognized as value. And you will also notice that something is often of more value to a person than we perceive it to be.

I was told by someone very smart that there are more people who think we are of value and will pay more for our value than we think they will pay.

So the lesson is simple. We exist to provide value plus help others recognize our value.

Air'n, it's time to close. For now I've given you four lessons. Let's look at them. Number one, think and grow rich. What the mind can believe and conceive it will achieve. Lesson two is the drive behind the drive. Lesson three is your winning formula. And lesson four is to give and recognize value.

Be a person who lives to create value. Have a great sleep.

Love, Your Uncle Joe."

Letter #3

"Air'n, I'm sitting in the Dallas Airport at Delta's terminal. My flight departs at 7:45 to Orlando and I thought this would be the perfect place to teach you the next lesson on how I make money.

Let's do a quick review of the first four lessons:

1. Your mind is a computer-like tool. Think and grow rich. Program in your affirmation of achievement.
2. Discover and embrace your drive behind your drive. Love this aspect of yourself completely.
3. We all have a shadow. Never doubt what you saw in the light when you are in the dark. Know your winning formula and know when money has pulled you into darkness.
4. Value. The more value you provide, the more money you make.

Lesson number five: Mentor your mentor's spirit.

One of my first mentors was Tom Hopkins. I was introduced to Tom Hopkins through a series of synchronistic events that shaped a lot of the direction of my life.

While I was selling real estate in 1976 on the south side of Chicago, a man came to our office to sell tickets to a training seminar for a man named Tom Hopkins. The day the man spoke at our sales meeting I was not present. However, my manager told me how this man came to the office, made a group presentation and sold tickets to individual agents to attend a Tom Hopkins seminar.

Then my manager said the words that changed my destiny: "Joe, you would really be good at selling seminar tickets." He gave me the business card of Jerry Sharp, the regional director for Tom Hopkins.

I went back to my desk with the words: "Joe, you would really be good at selling seminar tickets" in my mind. I picked up the phone and called Jerry Sharp. Jerry gave me his boss' phone number, a man named Mike Pinto. Mike and I met three weeks later at a coffee shop in Oaklawn, Illinois and Mike described to me what a career with Tom Hopkins Champions Unlimited would be like.

To make a long story short, I left real estate over the next 60 to 90 days and was now full-time with Hopkins.

Tom Hopkins was the protégé of a man named Jay Douglas Edwards. Jay was the guru for Realtors in the 1950s and 1960s who handed the mantle to Tommy. I loved this concept of being a guru and of being the best in the world and the most sought-after. Plus, when I went to my first Tom Hopkins seminar there were 1,000 people in the ballroom. All of them paid $200 to be there. That's $200,000. Then I watched Tommy sell 500 sets of tapes for $300 each for another $150,000. He just generated $350,000 in one day.

Air'n this is 1978 and $350,000 was a ton of money for a 21-year-old kid from the south side of Chicago to witness being paid.

Something happened that day. I had an experience of watching a master at work. Hopkins was so smooth, so polished and so powerful. He had complete control of everything.

When I met him for the first time, he made me feel like I was the only person in the room. He put his right hand on my shoulder and said, "That is a great tie. You look wonderful." It was so sincere, so genuine.

Air'n, what I saw after the event is what really lit the fire of desire. The entire sales team went up to Tom Hopkins' presidential suite after the program. I had never seen anything like it. And the way he looked... His Rolex, impeccable dress, and the most beautiful woman I had ever seen draped all over his arm. Tommy was my hero.

Over the next year I got some of the best learning of my life and you will shortly understand why I say, "Mentor the mentor's spirit, not their ego."

Whenever you see big money, success and a mentor's winning formula, remember that lesson. I was able to see Tommy Hopkins' winning formula and his shadow. It's not important that I detail what I saw. The important point is that I fell for the ego but I stayed for the spirit.

Whenever you choose a mentor, a guide or teacher remember that the things of the world that mentor has – money, power, prestige, sex – will seduce you. That's OK. The real mentoring begins when you discover their spirit.

The spirit is the real gift the guru gives. I watched thousands of people enter Tommy's presence and leave it more inspired. ("Inspired" literally means "to breathe spirit into.")

I knew that if I sold someone a ticket to his seminar, he would feel better about himself. Maybe for an hour, maybe for a day, a week or a lifetime. But what I learned from Hopkins was that when God wants to work through you then you have no choice. You simply are inspiring.

This lesson shaped a lot of my belief systems. I knew I could have money without having to be perfect behind the scenes yet give the illusion I was and still be inspiring. And make a difference in people's lives.

So the lesson is that as you seek gurus, teachers and mentors look at the inspiration they provide for others. Is it clean, clear and full of love? Don't look at the person; they have clay feet. Trust God, not people; they have egos, filled with fear.

Mentor the spirit of your mentor.

Love you, Uncle Joey

Letter #4

Air'n, I'm in Daytona Beach on a Sunday night. In 10 hours I'll be speaking to 350 to 400 agents and lenders here at the Adams Mark Resort. Every month for the past 10 years I have lead a three-day training called THE MAIN EVENT.

One of the great blessings in my life is when you traveled with me to Washington, DC for THE MAIN EVENT. You really impressed upon me the gifts you have: willingness, courage, adventure, kindness and humor. These characteristics are critical in making money. Hold to them tightly and share them, for everything you share makes you stronger.

Tonight I want to give you one of my most treasured insights about how I make money. It may seem paradoxical when you first hear it, but isn't most of life?

Lesson number six: To make money you must do it for free.

In 1983 when I decided to make speaking and coaching a career, I did what 9 out of 10 speakers do: I established a good, canned talk about three hours in length, made up a sales brochure and proceeded to market my three-hour talk/training. My class was "How to Handle Incoming Calls – Telephone Techniques."

I would call companies that were running ads on the radio, in newspapers and the Yellow Pages and act as if I was a potential client interested in their product or service. If I thought the person was poorly trained, I'd call the owner and offer my services. I'd offer to come in for three hours for $500 and train as many people as they wanted. I was fairly successful but not making big money, not like Tom Hopkins or Zig Ziglar, not even close. The best part about this start was that I got a lot of practice for a variety of different businesses.

My first big breakthrough idea came from my first wife, Cathy. Cathy at the time was selling Yellow Page advertising and she said, "Yellow Page advertising really works. It gets the phone to ring for the small business. The problem is that the person answering the phone doesn't know how to convert the caller to a customer." That one comment was the genesis of my first million-dollar business.

I said, "Cathy, if you could help make the Yellow Page advertiser more effective at handling incoming calls, would that increase trackable results for your clients? And if so, could you sell or renew more of your client advertising?" She answered with an enthusiastic "Yes!"

Her enthusiasm led me to the idea of approaching a man named Newton Arnold, who owned Arnold Advertising. At the time he was one of the larger independent Yellow Page advertisers in the Los Angeles area. I had the idea of him paying me $2,000 for a three-hour seminar for all of his clients who advertised in his books.

We tested the idea. We rented a ballroom and invited 100 people to attend a three-hour class called "It's For You – Your Most Important Call." To our amazement we 200 people showed up. The training was excellent.

Newton immediately asked me to schedule 10 more events over the next six months. Now I had $20,000 worth of business on the books and most importantly, some time to think how I could leverage the idea.

Can you see the lesson here? If you want to make money you must do it for free. What I discovered was that my training had great value to Newton, who could give it for free. Not that I did it for free; I found someone who would pay and then give it for free. Keep this thought in mind, because what was about to happen still gives me goose bumps.

One afternoon I was sitting in the warehouse of an office filled with Yellow Page books. At the time there were over 3,000 independent Yellow Page publishers, plus Nynex, Pac Bell, Bell Atlantic, Southwest Bell. All totaled over 10 million businesses used the Yellow Pages at the time.

I thought if I could produce an audio tape that I could sell to all Yellow Page advertisers, I would have a potential market of 10 million buyers. Immediately I got to work on producing the tape.

When it was done, it was masterful! I invested about $5,000 in the production of a super-high-quality 60-minute training tape. Newton Arnold loved the tape so much he bought 5,000 copies. As an extra added value, I had Newton record a message in his voice at the beginning of the tape, thanking his clients for advertising in his book.

Well Ron Schindler, owner of Schindler Publishing in Louisville, Kentucky, talked to Newton and ordered 5,000 copies. Then something miraculous happened. I got several calls from small businesses around the Louisville area asking me if I could send them a copy of the tape. And now I was selling the tape for $10.

I was a bit perplexed by this because I wasn't sure how they were finding out about the tape. Then one day a limousine company sent me a little newspaper clipping that read, "New audio tape is helping Yellow Page advertisers become much more effective when calls come from Yellow Page clients. Schindler Publishing is giving the tape away for free." Then it had my phone number.

This was a little free publicity ad Schindler ran in a small Louisville newspaper. Here is how I leveraged the idea. I made 500 copies of the newspaper article. Then I wrote a personal note on each article that said, "Bob (or Sandy or whomever), the owner of the Yellow Page company was pleased to find out more about this tape. We should give them to our customers." I hand-addressed 500 envelopes with no return address and sent them to the 500 publishers.

In the next six months we sold 1,000,000 copies of the tape to about 100 different publishers, including Nynex, Pac Bell, Bell Atlantic, who gave it to their clients for free.

What a great lesson! I have used this principal all my business life: Find a way to give it away.

Air'n, so far you have six lessons on how I make money:

1. Think and grow rich.
2. Know your drive behind the drive.
3. Know your winning formula.
4. Add value, then more value.
5. Mentor your mentor's spirit.
6. Give it away to make money.

Sleep well.

Love, Uncle Joey

Letter #5

I'm sitting at Starbucks in Daytona Beach by myself writing you this letter.

Lesson number seven: Be a journaler.

You've seen me writing in my journal for years. I always carry my journal with me to capture thoughts, make notes of ideas and write letters that may or may not ever get read.

Most recently my journal has been my therapist. Since April 29, 2002, I have written over 100 letters to Manna, some expressing my anger, my ambivalence, my hate, my care, my loss and recently my forgiveness, my letting go and now my joy. When you can write your emotions in the form of a letter, you can easily communicate exactly what's on your mind. Manna will never see the letters; my journals have been a place for me to process.

Air'n, journaling is a way of cleaning your mind by dumping all your thoughts onto paper. When you were at my apartment last month I showed you all the stacks of my journals.

I have over 115 journals filled with thoughts, doodles, ideas, letters, book reviews, telephone conversations and all types of notes.

Most importantly, a journal is a place for you to center yourself. A safe haven. A place where you can talk to God. I have my journal next to me right now. I'm looking at my recent entries. What I see are my notes from my readings. I'm deep in the study in *The Course in Miracles*. I'm listening to it on tape. I'm also reading the book simultaneously. When an inspiring passage occurs, I stop the recorder and write the thought in my journal, then have a conversation in print with myself.

Air'n, the journal has become my way of having a relationship with me. My journal is my best friend, because my journal is me.

Now how will this help you make money? Air'n, making money is thinking clearly and relating cleanly to money. When you have a journal to write out your thoughts and you can see how clear your relationship is with yourself, you'll make a lot of money.

So the lesson in this letter is be a journaler.

Love,
Your Uncle Joe.

Letter #6

Good morning Air'n! I'm sitting in the passenger seat of a tour bus early Saturday morning with Jim, Dean, Kevin, Mike and myself. We are on what is called "The Trent Jones Tour." This is a golf tour through Alabama. Trent Jones was a very famous golfer who built many courses in the south. So we decided to take a 10-day bus tour to play 10 rounds of golf.

Golf is one of those things you want to master, because it appears so easy yet it's so difficult. I've been playing for 13 years and seriously for about six years, yet I've only improved slightly. I still shoot in the 90s with an occasional 80. My lowest score ever was an 82 at my country club Morgan Run.

Golf is a great acronym to describe how to organize a project, organize a day, organize an activity and even organize a life.

Dean Jackson invented this thought and I want to share it with you.

G is for **G**oal. Create a very specific goal that you can dedicate three to four uninterrupted hours to. I love the morning time, from 5am to 8am. The mind seems to really focus. One has a limited amount of time and a specific, predetermined outcome.

The **O** stands for having only **O**ne thing on your mind. Single-mindedness creates whole-mindedness. When golfing, you eliminate all distractions because you're isolated from outside influence.

To get really high-quality thinking done create a space where your mind can operate on one thing for three hours and watch the magic appear. Whenever I'm creating a new thought process, working on a book, a course or a class and I have three uninterrupted hours the state of flow comes into being.

And then **L** stands for **L**imited time. Action fills the time that it's given. Limited time means more urgency and more urgency means more focus.

I've noticed that I play much better golf when we play at a fairly brisk pace. I think the mind has less time to wander and worry and get into trouble on its own.

Recently Dean and I created a complete marketing program with 12 different components. Each time we sat down, we first set a goal to eliminate all distractions and choose only one thing to work on. We created a limited amount of time and then focused every part of our thinking to accomplish that goal.

Finally the **F** is for **F**ocus. When you bring your attention to one thing without any distortion, distraction or a divided mind, the ability to achieve your goal is remarkable.

Air'n, taking 60 minutes a day to write to you is GOLF. I have a goal, only one thing, a limited time and extreme focus.

As I look back over the body of work that I've created in my lifetime – my powerful telephone prospecting techniques, the 60-Minute Business Plan, the Guerrilla Marketing Program, the Getting Tough Album, the Level Selling System, the Taking Control: 30 Days To Greatness Program, the Relationship Marketing Program, the Drip Campaign, the Next Time Campaign, the Power Referral Programs, THE MAIN EVENT, www.byreferralonly.com, Live Coaching – it's a massive body of work, books, tapes and videos that are a direct result of GOLF. Have a goal, a limited amount of time, only one focus and focus extremely on that.

So far I have shared with you seven life lessons that I have learned. Number one is think and grow rich. The one choice you'll always have in life is what thought you want to think. You can either think your thought or the thought thinks you. Practice, practice, practice. Strengthen your mind. Think your thoughts. Don't let your thoughts think you.

Number two: Know the drive behind the drive. I love to find ways to strengthen my ability to motivate myself to change. Change your mind. It sounds easy. And it is if you have a drive behind the drive.

Air'n you have the intelligence, you have the IQ and you have the personality. Now, reach inside and spark the drive behind the drive.

Number three: Know your winning formula. Air'n, listen closely to people who speak. When they are under pressure, they reveal their winning formula. Pressure has a way of revealing reality. Under pressure, coal can become a diamond. Under pressure, orange juice flows from an orange. Under pressure, whatever is really inside comes out.

Number four: Bring value to others. You are paid in direct proportion to the value others believe they are receiving from you.

Number five: Mentor the mentor's spirit. The Holy Spirit is that blessing you receive when you set your self-interest apart. Whenever you are as interested in others as you are in yourself, the Holy Spirit is present. Regardless of the professional direction you choose Air'n, you will be a teacher. Teach only love. Drive fear out. Only love.

Love comes through the Holy Spirit. When you are truly interested in having all, give all. That is the first lesson in *The Course in Miracles*.

Lesson number six: Give it away for free. A thought that is shared is strengthened. A thought that is not shared is weakened. Therefore if you want something in your thought system to weaken and lessen its grip on your mind, then stop sharing it. Like my divorce. When I share about it, it strengthens. When I don't share it, entertain it, think about it or analyze it, it weakens.

Air'n, find things in your life that you want to strengthen and share. And share it for free. The money will always follow.

Lesson number seven: Be a journaler. Start now Air'n. Journal your journey. A life worth living is a life worth recording. Knowing what I know now, I would have been journaling much earlier in my life.

And number eight: GOLF. Clear goals, only one thing, limited time and full focus.

It's taken me 46 years to figure all this out. My only wish for you is that you take what I'm sharing to heart, blend it in with all of your other reading and life experiences and use it to create a full, peaceful, rich life.

Love, Your Uncle Joe.

Letter #7

This is our fifth day on our golf trip through the Robert Trent Jones trails. It's been a magnificent example of how money can be wisely invested so everyone benefits.

The State of Alabama set up a retirement fund for teachers. They've invested that money in 10 or 12 golf courses throughout the state. It looks like the McDonalds franchise of clubhouses. They're all identical. The courses are all designed by Robert Trent Jones. They're extraordinary designs. We're staying in hotels along the way that all have a similar look and feel. I've never experienced such a well-planned, well-thought-out golf system in my life. This is the theme of this letter.

The system is the solution. The words were spoken to me from a book called *The E-Myth* by Michael Gerber. Check out his Web site Emyth.com.

What a system does is provide consistent, reliable, predictable results. The design of a system starts with first designing the purpose of a life.

"What is my primary aim in life?" This might be the single, most important question you ask yourself as you begin to grow your business. Another way to ask this question is, "What do you want your life to look like, day by day?"

Start by designing your perfect day Air'n. Then design a business that will provide as many perfect days as possible.

Here's an example of what a perfect day looks like for me. It begins early at 6am with prayer. "God, I put my trust in you today. My calling is to serve. Help me today to be a better servant for you. Help me today to look for the good in myself and others, in all situations, and find it. Help me God to live only for today and to live this day as if it were my last."

This takes about a minute. And it's my way of asking for direction.

Second, I like to meditate. Meditation is one of those actions that the mind hates. The mind wants to get moving, thinking, engaged. The Buddha calls it "the monkey mind." Watch a monkey. He will grab onto anything that's in front of him. The mind works the same way. It grabs a thought and hangs onto it.

Meditation is a way to bring detachment. I sit in my meditation room while I'm home or on a pillow when I'm on the road. I breathe deeply. It's called triangle breathing. You breathe deeply for five seconds, you hold for five seconds, and then you release for five seconds. I like to do this 10 times, at which point my mind slows down and I fix on a word *shante* which means peace.

I say it slowly, 100 times. That is called a mantra. Peace of mind. My total meditation takes about 15 minutes. It's the wind in my sail. When I miss my meditation, I feel it all day. If I miss two days, people around me notice that I've missed it. I'm more fearful, more anxious and feel more isolated when I miss my meditation.

Prayer and meditation early in the morning are a big secret to how I make money. Prayer and meditation is asking for direction and listening for the direction to come from the highest part of yourself; what I like to call the Holy Spirit.

The third thing I do is yoga. I discovered yoga in 1996. I was going through the breakup of my first marriage. At that time, I met a very powerful and very peaceful woman who lived below me in the condominium complex. Her name was Perry Ness.

Perry invited me to come to her yoga studio, which was just a two-minute walk from where we lived. The class is 90 minutes long.

I just remembered you did a class with me recently. It's a deep, deep sweat. I get this detoxification of all old memory and old cigar smoke and all the other impurities that might be in my body.

I've really fallen in love with this form of exercise. As I write to you right now, it's been 12 days since I've taken this class and I miss it so much. I miss it almost as much as seeing my daughters, Tracy and Olivia. That's how much it means to me.

The fourth thing I like to do is listen to books on tape. I love to sit on my deck from 8:30 in the evening until about 10pm and listen to great authors read their books.

There's a wonderful Web site called Audible.com and another one called Nightingale.com I use with my Ipod. Those three things have become some of the most important learning resources in my life. When I engage my mind in a direct way, with my journal and my Ipod, I can get completely absorbed in a state of flow.

To make money I must constantly be learning and I learn best by listening.

The fifth thing I like to do in my ideal day is teach, collaborate and coach. Teaching is my way of learning. I love to teach what I am learning. I'm fascinated with new ways of thinking. I love new ideas. I love the excitement my learners experience when they hear me share my insights, my awarenesses and my ideas.

I love the 3½ hours on stage in the role of teacher when I travel around the country conducting my free workshops. It's like the whole experience fills me up with inspiration. I get lost in the message and often don't even know what I'm going to say until I say it.

The best thing about my life is I've been blessed with a business that has a system of teaching these half-day seminars five to eight times a month. The travel is sometimes a grind but I am willing to pay the price for those 3½ hours on stage. I used to think the adrenaline that I got was an addiction. Today I know that teaching is my calling. So teaching is as important to me as breathing.

You can create a business that allows you to use your unique ability Air'n. Read Dan Sullivan's book *Focusing on Your Unique Ability.* Your joy level for life will soar.

Now, the sixth thing I love to do is coach. Coaching is helping people with very specific challenges in life and in business. As I've had great personal coaches in my life, I know the value the role plays.

Jay Abraham coached me for a few years in his methods of marketing. He actually gave me the concept of the coaching club. My first coaching service was called VMAP. That's Voice Mail Accountability Program. I would assign a voice mailbox to a person. They were to leave me a voicemail with any questions they had. Then when I had time, I would respond by leaving a message for them with my advice and coaching. At one time, I had 50 people paying me $150 a month to be part of this service. I loved it.

It was the genesis of my current company BY REFERRAL ONLY. Today we coach over 3,000 people who pay $299 a month. I invest anywhere from 5 to 10 hours a week on the phone, coaching one-on-one and in small group TeleClasses.

The seventh thing I like to do is collaborate. This has been the area of my life most in flux. Today I collaborate with many good friends. We are in the infancy of creating new ideas, new thoughts and new collaborations. I love to be at the center of contact with brilliant men and women around the world who share and learn what is new and how to put a new spin on what is old.

I always carry with me a list of 20 people who I want to meet over the next three to five years and want to collaborate with. My recent list looks like this: number one is Marianne Williamson, the author of *Return to Love*. Gerald Jablonski, Al Reese, Jim Bunch, Michael Gerber, Ken Blanchard, Bill Hybill, John Maxwell, Jack Canfield, Wayne Dyer, Bill Bacharach, Byron Katie, Joe Jowarski, Dan Sullivan and Eckhart Tolle who wrote a wonderful book called *The Power Of Now*. Peter Drucker and Gary Keller who own one of the largest real estate companies in North America. Perry Ness and Carolyn Myss.

Creating a list like this is something I've been doing for years. How I will connect with these people is not certain. What is certain is I will.

Air'n the two things that will change and evolve you more than any other are the people you allow to influence you and the environment you create for yourself. That is why I always say to you, "The reason you're at the University of Southern California going to school right now is to meet people."

The real secret to having your list of people to collaborate with is even if you never meet any of them, you condition your mind to accept yourself as a person worthy and valuable enough to be in their life and them in yours.

Relationships like the ones that I have had with Thomas Leonard and Brian Tracy and Gary Rossberg and Jay Abraham and Vic Conant were all somewhat serendipitous. But it all started by putting their name on a list.

Now the eighth activity that fits into my ideal day is golf. I just love golf. I love being outside. I love being in the sunshine. I love the trees, the grass, the water. Mostly, I love the way the game challenges me to stay present. I want to play this the rest of my life.

And then the ninth activity is time with Olivia and Tracy. Olivia is nine. She's evolving into a funny, extroverted, authentic, vulnerable, smart person. My time with her is filled with joy.

Tracy is 16 and getting ready to get her first car. She's also a gift. Tracy calls me every day, because she knows my hearing her voice is magic.

So Air'n my primary aim is to live with these activities: prayer, meditation, yoga, listen to books on tape with my Ipod, teach, coach, collaborate, golf and be a dad to Olivia and Tracy.

I've created a business system that allows me to spend almost all of my days with seven or eight out of these nine activities. Once you have your primary aim, creating the business comes second. I like to teach it this way. First design the life you want, then put your business inside the life.

Love, Your Uncle Joe.

P.S. Do what you love and the money will follow.

I loved sharing my letters to Air'n with you. And I'm curious what value you received from this book.

That's it. My best thinking on getting focused, staying focused, helping focus others and focusing on money.

My intention was to bring you value for the time that you've invested with me. I wish you full hearted focus.

So tell me if you recognize the value that you've received from this book. You can do that by sending me an email to JoeStumpf@gmail.com

About Joe Stumpf

Joe Stumpf has been in and around the real estate coaching and training business since 1977.

In 1981, he started his training and coaching company, which has grown to be one of the largest coaching companies in North America.

Joe Stumpf has a subscription-based company with over 5,000 clients, the purpose of which is to teach the principles, provide the tools and systems, to be highly profitable and at the same time serve others with the heart of a "Super Servant".

Joe Stumpf invests most of his time and energy in creating, writing, and video/audio recording, while his leadership team runs his company's day-to-day operations. His work has been a wonderful vehicle to express his creativity, as through it he gets to live a life fully expressed as a model of possibility.

It is the perfect forum for him to discover and allow his most authentic self to be publicly shared.In all of Joe Stumpf's work his intention is to create the next version of himself, one which is more aligned with his soul-purpose.

He has gained a sense of mastery on the goal line while maintaining a sense of sacred purpose.

Reading, writing, teaching, and coaching is woven into his fabric.

He possesses a beautiful coaching gift of being able to channel insight and awareness to people when they seek clarity and direction in business and life. He helps people in profound ways so they can experience the shifts they desire as a result of crossing his path.

He views this as his life's purpose.

You're welcome to take a closer look at Joe's work at MyByreferralOnly.com or you can write to Joe at JoeStumpf@gmail.com.

Made in the USA
San Bernardino, CA
27 August 2014